"Sharks on the Loose!"

Kathryn White
Illustrated by Andy Elkerton

OXFORD

Chapter 1 – Sharks on the prowl

The sharks saw their prey.

They waited and watched as the group of children moved closer and closer. The sharks' hungry eyes looked for a chance to attack. The children stayed packed together, like a shoal of sardines. Then one kid waved her arm. The sharks' eyes lit up.

Yes, there would be blood.

Yes, there would be screams.

The sharks knew there would be no mercy. They'd attack at speed and then vanish before they could be caught.

No one would ever know what happened.

No one would ever find them.

Time to move in.

Time to attack …

Leo peered through the gaps in the shark's rubber teeth. Matt, Leo's best friend, tried not to giggle at the weird sight of Leo's eyes peering out of his shark mouth.

But Matt was having a worse time. He was taller than Leo, so his shark's teeth kept poking up his nose.

Leo and Matt were wearing giant shark suits to advertise FELINI'S FANTASTIC FISH BAR. The boys had agreed to do it because Mr Felini was Leo's dad, and business was bad. Since McHaddock's opened in town selling fish nuggets at half price, Mr Felini had lost a lot of customers.

"I wanted to wear a Spiderman suit and be a superhero," Matt sneezed.

"Felini's doesn't sell soup for spiders. It sells fish soup," said Leo flatly.

"Maybe Spiderman eats fish soup," said Matt.

"Duh, everyone knows Spiderman eats fly soup," joked Leo. The boys laughed.

That's when they saw Rosa and her pals. They were some kids who'd got Max and Leo into trouble at school last week. Leo's toothy eyes lit up.

"Time to get 'em back!"

FELIN
FANTAS
FISH
BAR

Chapter 2 – Shark attack!

The two rubber sharks shot out from behind the bush that masked them.

"Surprise!" shouted Matt.

"No mercy!" cried Leo as the disguised duo dived into the screaming group.

"SHARK!" squealed Rosa.

"Aaaarrgh! It's biting my leg," Ellie hollered. Matt locked Ellie's leg between both shark fins. He was snorting and chomping, pretending to bite it off.

"Poke the shark in the eye," shouted Adam as he shot off in his wheelchair. "It won't see where you are then."

"Human, prepare to meet your end!" yelled Leo, with Rosa's arm between his fins.

Suddenly something hit Leo's fins with a wallop. "Let her go!" shouted an old lady as she came round the corner.

"Uh?" Leo felt another thud through his thick rubber suit.

"Yes, you," said the lady, swinging her handbag at Leo. "Or I'll turn those fins into fish fingers."

Rosa snapped, "Leo Felini, I know it's you, you maggot," and pushed Leo straight into Matt.

Leo pulled the shark suit above his knees and made a run for it, with Matt close behind.

"Get them!" said the lady. "Show them it takes more than a couple of sharks to scare us girls."

Leo couldn't see where he was going, but he ran as fast as he could. He could hear the crowd behind him shouting, "Catch the sharks!"

Then **WHAM**, Leo smashed into a bus stop.

THUD, Matt ran into Leo and flattened him to the post.

Just then the No. 27 bus arrived. "Quick!" cried Matt. "Get on the bus." They bounced onto the bus, seconds before Rosa and the crowd raced up to the stop. Leo and Matt waved goodbye with a cheeky fin as the bus moved off.

Chapter 3 – Fare play

Leo and Matt wobbled. Neither could bend to sit down. At the next stop the driver frowned and tapped his ticket machine.

"Two sharks to the town centre, please," said Leo.

"Never had sharks on the bus before. Are you young or old sharks?" asked the driver.

"Half-price sharks," Matt said quickly.

The driver raised an eyebrow and held up the tickets. Leo didn't have any money.

"Matt, please pay the driver," said Leo politely.

"Huh? Me?" Matt tried to get his hands out of his fins and into his trouser pocket but they were stuck tight.

Leo smiled sweetly at the driver. "My shark friend won't be a minute. He's just got a minor fin problem."

Matt continued wrestling in his suit. Finally, Leo turned to the driver. "Would you help my friend, please? His fin is stuck and he can't get the money out."

"That's it," said the driver. "Off my bus. Go on, beat it."

"But I *have* got the money," said Matt, sweating and panting.

"That's a shark's tale. Catch the next boat," said the driver.

Matt and Leo hopped down onto the pavement and watched the bus drive off.

By the time Matt and Leo waddled into the shopping mall, they were hot and tired.

"I need something ice cold," said Matt.

Then Leo's eyes lit up like light bulbs. Two giant ice cream cones were walking towards them. "I can't believe my eyes," said Leo. "Huge, delicious ice cream cones!"

Matt gave Leo a strange look. "You dingbat," he said. "They're not real ice cream cones."

"Duh! I know. They're O'Neil's ice creams. Joe O'Neil must be advertising his mum's business. Which means?" said Leo.

"Free ice cream!" said Matt, licking his lips.

The sharks cruised up to the ice cream cones. All they could see of Joe were his two bright green, cheeky eyes.

"Joe, are we glad to see you!" said Matt. "Any chance of some free ice cream? These sharks are gasping!"

The big green eyes peering from the ice cream cone narrowed.

"Oh, come on, Joe," Leo begged.
"I'll make a deal. You wanted to borrow my
rubber spider to hide in Hayley's school bag,
remember? Well, I'll bring it in on Monday."

The big green eyes sparkled with delight
and winked at the other ice cream cone.

"Is it a deal?" grinned Leo.

The ice cream cone gave the thumbs up and
led the boys into O'Neil's Ice cream Parlour.

While the sharks polished off their ice cream, Mrs O'Neil moaned about McHaddock's serving cheap ice cream and stealing her customers.

"That ice cream was cool, Joe – ice cool!" joked Leo. "So it's a deal. One scary spider in Hayley's bag on Monday."

Suddenly Matt gave Leo a nudge. Joe O'Neil wasn't in the ice cream suit at all. In fact, Joe had just walked into the ice cream parlour.

"Great shark suits," said Joe.

A chill ran down Leo's back. "So who's disguised as an ice cream cone making deals with me?" he thought in horror.

The vanilla ice cream cone slowly lifted its scoop. There, standing underneath with a look of triumph, was Hayley, Joe's sister.

"Better watch *your* school bag!" sneered Hayley.

"Yeah, too right. The mask has slipped," said the other ice cream cone, revealing Hayley's best friend, Mia.

"Whoa, let's go!" shouted Leo and both sharks dived out of the parlour.

Joe and his mum laughed as both ice cream cones chased after the sharks shouting, "Think we're scared of spiders, eh?"

O'NEIL'S
ICE CRE

21

The sharks raced through the shopping mall followed by the giant ice cream cones. They had almost reached the street when they saw Rosa and her crowd coming towards them.

"Get 'em!" shouted Rosa.

Matt and Leo dived into Max Spenders Department Store and ran through the shoe area.

"Sharks!" cried a salesman, hopping onto a footstool.

Sharks!

SHOE SALE

O'NEIL'S ICE CREAM

O'NEIL'S ICE CR

Matt and Leo bumbled into the lift. The lift doors closed just before the security guards reached them. Rosa and her crowd were already fishing for Matt and Leo on the computer games floor. The hunt was on.

The lift stopped. "Now what are we going to do?" said Matt.

An announcement came through the store speakers: "Security to ground floor. Emergency. We have two giant ice cream cones on the loose."

"Phew!" said Leo. "They'll create a bit of a distraction. Let's hide!"

"Oh, yeah? And where can a pair of rubber sharks hide?" said Matt.

Leo smiled. "I know just the place."

The toy department was full of lively toddlers. They pushed the sharks onto the floor and used them as bouncy castles.

"Help!" said Matt. "I'm drowning!"

The sharks got up and dived for cover in the netted ballpark. Both disappeared under the balls as toddlers jumped in after them like lemmings. Rosa and her crowd raced past them twice – but didn't notice them.

The gasping sharks struggled free and escaped down a back staircase. They made it outside and waddled towards the river bridge that led home.

"I've had enough of this suit," panted Matt.

"Yeah," nodded Leo. "Let's get home, wriggle out of them and become us again."

But when they got to the bridge, they heard screams. A woman, clutching her little girl's hand, was calling for help. The little girl had let go of their puppy's lead and the puppy had dived into the river to play with the ducks. It couldn't swim and was splashing helplessly around in the deep water.

"Pirate's going to drown!" cried the little girl desperately.

The sharks clambered down to the river. "Don't worry, we'll save him!" said Leo.

"What?" said Matt. "Are you crazy? We'll be the ones who drown in these shark suits!"

But Leo had already dived in with a mighty splash. Would his shark suit weigh him down? Would he sink to the bottom? Matt held his breath and waited.

Suddenly he saw a shark fin and Leo floated to the surface like a giant rubber raft. Matt breathed a sigh of relief and dived in too.

By now a crowd was shouting from the bridge, "Sharks in the river!"

Within minutes, newspaper reporters had arrived and cameras were clicking.

The two sharks paddled in circles, closing in on the struggling pup. Matt and Leo tried to stay calm but the puppy kept disappearing below the surface. It took longer each time to come up.

"Boy, that's one weird sight!" said the reporters. "Two sharks and a puppy in the river!"

Leo then dived underneath the sinking puppy. Seconds later up he came with Pirate lying on the belly of his suit! The riverbank of people cheered.

"I feel as light as a jellyfish," said Leo, paddling around triumphantly. The exhausted puppy rested happily on top of the rubber shark suit.

"Yeah, this rocks!" said Matt, floating by his side.

By the time the sharks returned Pirate to shore, the local TV news team was there.

"They saved Pirate," the little girl told them. "I love sharks!"

"Ah, it was nothing," said Matt. "That's what disguised superheroes do!"

Mr Felini arrived, puffed up with pride. "These boys have been great sports for advertising Felini's," he told reporters. "And now I've got more publicity for my fish bar than I could ever have dreamed of. Hey boys, how about octopus suits next week?"